# Dancing in Soot

Richard Brown
Illustrated by Patrice Aggs

CAMBRIDGE
UNIVERSITY PRESS

When I was little, my grandad owned a small farm, which was near our house. There was a stable, a corn house and a dovecote to explore. There was an orchard to run through and two gates to climb over.

Chickens scratched about, and a pig called Sally grunted in the sun. It was a mucky place, with mud, hay, chickens' droppings and bags of soot that leant against the orchard hedge. I loved the farm and so did my little brother David.

Across the road from the farm there was a meadow. Once a year it would suddenly fill with the noise, the lights and the magic of a fair.

The day of the fair was an exciting time for the whole family.

Grandad, Mum and Dad, Aunt Dinah, Uncle Bill and Uncle Freddy all turned up in their best clothes, and we all went off to the fair.

Before the fair, there was a procession through the town. I was often chosen to be a princess on a float. There were three other princesses too, and there was a queen. David was one of the page-boys.

We rode through the village on a lorry decorated with leaves and flowers. I used to feel so excited. So did David.

One year, Mum made sure that my white dress was ironed and spotless and my crown of flowers was just right. On the day of the fair, she dressed me in front of the tall mirror in her bedroom. She watched proudly as I twirled about and giggled.

I couldn't wait to get to the fair.

"Now," said Mum, "I've got you two ready early so that I don't have to bother with you while I get myself ready. You go and wait for us outside. I don't want you getting under everyone's feet. We shan't be long. And remember, please make quite sure that you keep your shoes and socks clean. Do you understand?"

We looked at our shoes and socks and we both nodded. “Of course we will,” I said.

Every room in the house seemed to be full of uncles, aunts and grandparents getting ready to go to the fair. They laughed, tried on hats, tied ties and smoothed back hair. David and I were glad to go outside to get away from all the noise and fuss.

It was very quiet outside. We walked up the lane to Grandad's farm. We wandered about for a while, too scared to do anything in case our shoes and socks got muddy.

We could see the fair over the road and we watched it for a while.

Then we got bored. Why didn't the grown-ups hurry up?

I said to David, "Let's take our shoes and socks off, then they won't get muddy."

David was younger than me, so he copied me. We pulled off our shoes and socks, giggling as our bare feet touched the cold ground.

We put our shoes and socks carefully near the gate to the lane.

"They won't get muddy here," I said.

Now, at last, we were free to play.

David wandered about a bit and I played with Sally, the pig. She liked to have her back scratched.

Then David called me over to the hedge and said, “What’s this?”

There was a pile of sacks. Some of the sacks had burst and were spilling soot onto the yard.

"I've seen Grandad put this on the fields," I said.

We poked our fingers into it. It was black, and it felt like flour.

David wiped his fingers on the sack, and this gave us an idea. We smeared soot on our arms and faces. We pretended to be clowns.

Then I stuck my toes into the soot and did a wild little dance, waving my arms about and making funny noises.

David joined in, and the soot flew around. We had the time of our lives.

Soon we were covered with soot. It got everywhere, in our ears, our eyes, our hair. My lovely white dress was filthy. I began to feel a bit ashamed of myself.

"What will Mum say?" said David.

That made me feel worse, so I said, "She only told us to keep our socks and shoes clean. Well, they are. Look!" And I pointed to our shoes and socks.

Our shoes and socks were spotless. “Come on,” I said. “Let’s go back now.”

We left a trail of sooty footprints all down the lane to our back door.

We were just about to put down our shoes and socks when the back door flew open. There stood Mum. She stared at us in horror.

Suddenly, I felt very small and silly and very, very dirty. I wiped some soot from my eye. Mum was furious! We just stood there, trembling.

We were bundled into the kitchen and told to take off our sooty clothes. I tried to say to Mum, “We did what you said. We kept our shoes and socks clean.” But she never gave me a chance.

We had to try to wash ourselves in a tin bath. The water got very dirty with soot. David began to cry. Then Mum got on her knees and soaped us both down, rubbing us hard until our skins glowed. She was still very angry.

"In less than an hour, you're supposed to be on that float," said Mum. "I'm not at all sure that you'll be allowed to go to the fair. Now, you can both go to your room. How am I going to get your clothes clean in time? Tell me that."

We hung our heads. Not go to the fair?

One of the worst moments was when we had to walk out of the kitchen, down the hall and up the stairs, wrapped in our towels.

Grandad, Aunt Dinah, Uncle Bill and Uncle Freddy were all there watching us, laughing or tut-tutting or shaking their heads, making us feel worse than ever. It wasn't fair.

Halfway up the stairs I stopped. I turned round to them all and shouted, “It’s not fair! We kept our shoes and socks clean just as we promised.”

But that just made them laugh even more. Mum shooed us up the stairs.

David and I shivered in our underclothes. We didn't know whether to get dressed.

I felt terrible. What would happen now?

It was too late for anyone to take our places on the float. Everyone would know that something had happened to us. What if they found out what we had done? David had stopped crying, but now *I* wanted to cry.

Mum came in. David said, "Can I go to the fair, Mum? *Please?*"

Mum frowned. "You don't deserve to, son, but it's more your sister's fault. Here, put this clean shirt on, and your other pair of long trousers. Your bow tie is all right. I think we'll just about manage."

David looked so happy then. But what about me?

“As for you, my girl,” said Mum, “you can’t wear a different dress. It would look very odd beside the other princesses. I’m not sure that you’ll be able to go.”

I was left alone then. No princess. No float. No fair. I couldn’t believe it.

And then I heard Mum and Aunt Dinah outside.
I looked and saw the funniest sight.

First Mum, then Aunt Dinah, was running around the back yard with my dress, flapping it about in the air. They had washed it and now they were trying to get it dry.

"It's still damp," said Aunt Dinah a little later.

"It'll just have to dry on you," said Mum.

It did feel a bit damp, but I didn't care. I was so relieved. I was going to be a princess after all.

"Your crown's a bit dusty," said Grandad, smiling. "But your shoes and socks are just perfect."

"Silly girl," said Mum. "Now it's time to go."

And we all set off for the fair.